D1577554

The Rosary

Juliette Levivier

Illustrations by Anne Gravier

CTS Children's Books

Table of Contents

A crown for Mary

The Virgin Mary is Jesus' mother. Before he died on the cross, he gave her to us to be our mother. So she is your mother too; your mother in heaven.

She invites you to pray with her, thinking about different moments in Jesus' life. Mary knows her son so well that she can help you to look at him, pray to him and love him.

When you pray the rosary you are united with all the other people, near or far away, who are praying to Mary at the same time as you.

The name 'rosary' can make you think of a crown of roses. Imagine the beautiful crown that is on Mary's head thanks to your prayer!

Do you want to give Mary your hand so that she can lead you to Jesus through the rosary?

The mysteries of the rosary

What does 'mystery' mean?
Is it something you can't understand? No.
Is it something secret? No.
Is it something really complicated? No.
A mystery is something very precious which you discover bit by bit and understand a little more each day.

The mysteries of the rosary are important moments in Jesus' life which we think about together with Mary to be able to understand them better.

If you look at pages 14-15, 22-23, 30-31 and 38-39, you'll see they're like a summary of the Gospel.

There are four sets of mysteries in the rosary.
There are five mysteries in each set.
Each mystery is one decade of the rosary.
Each rosary has five decades of *Hail Marys*.
Each decade is ten *Hail Marys*.

When you pray

When you pray, take your time.
The important thing is not that you say a lot;
it's that you pray with Jesus and Mary and that
you let the Presence of God come into you.

When you pray, keep still. Whether you kneel
or sit, your body is praying too.

You can decide before you start whether you
want to pray a whole rosary or just one decade

Begin by reading the title of the mystery
and look at the drawing. Then slowly read the
verses from the Bible. Praying means looking
at Jesus. In silence imagine the scene. What is
Jesus saying? What is he doing? Who is he with?
Where is he?

Then read the little text which is there to help
you to ask a grace from Jesus and Mary. You
can use the one in the book or you can make up
your own.

 Calmly say one *Our Father* and
ten *Hail Marys* then one *Glory Be*. To
finish, you can read the prayer at the
bottom of the page.

When you pray
the rosary

You begin by making the sign of the cross. This puts you in the presence of God who loves you.

'In the name of the Father and of the Son and of the Holy Spirit. Amen.'

I believe in God,
the Father almighty,
creator of heaven and earth.
I believe in Jesus Christ, his only Son, our Lord.
He was conceived by the power of the Holy Spirit
and born of the Virgin Mary.
He suffered under Pontius Pilate,
was crucified, died, and was buried.
He descended to the dead.
On the third day he rose again.
He ascended into heaven,
and is seated at the right hand of the Father.
He will come again to judge the living
and the dead.
I believe in the Holy Spirit,
the holy Catholic Church,
the communion of saints,
the forgiveness of sins,
the resurrection of the body,
and life everlasting.
Amen.

Our Father, who art in heaven,
hallowed be thy name.
Thy kingdom come.
Thy will be done on earth as it is in heaven.
Give us this day our daily bread,
and forgive us our trespasses,
as we forgive those who trespass against us,
and lead us not into temptation,
but deliver us from evil.
Amen.

Hail, Mary, full of grace,
the Lord is with thee:
blessed art thou among women,
and blessed is the fruit of thy womb, Jesus.
Holy Mary, mother of God,
pray for us sinners,
now, and at the hour of our death.
Amen.

Glory be to the Father,
and to the Son and to the Holy Spirit.
As it was in the beginning,
is now, and ever shall be,
world without end.
Amen.

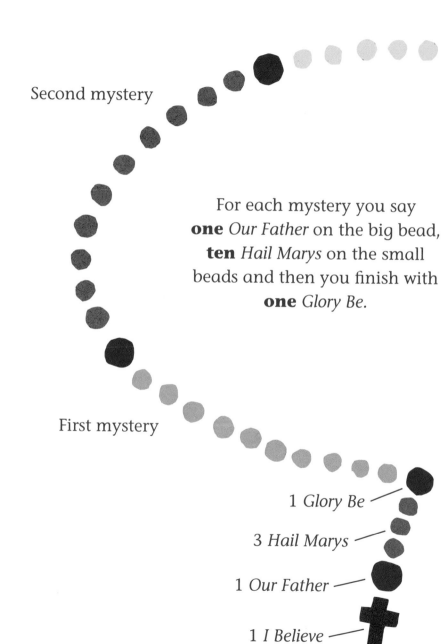

Second mystery

For each mystery you say
one *Our Father* on the big bead,
ten *Hail Marys* on the small
beads and then you finish with
one *Glory Be.*

10

First mystery

1 *Glory Be*

3 *Hail Marys*

1 *Our Father*

1 *I Believe*

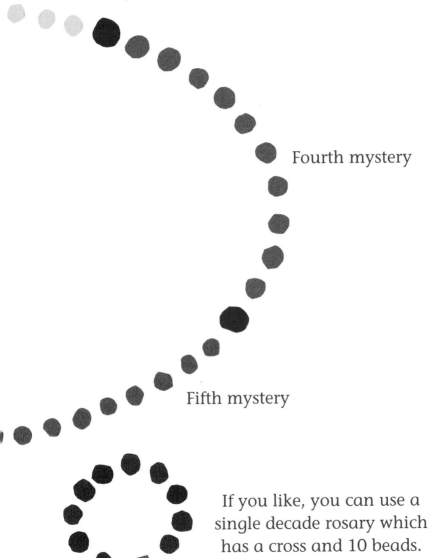

Third mystery

Fourth mystery

Fifth mystery

II

If you like, you can use a single decade rosary which has a cross and 10 beads.

Praying with th

Every day, Christians
all over the world say the rosary.
You can join them!

Choose your day...

ildren of the world

Mondays and Saturdays
the joyful mysteries

Thursdays
the mysteries of light

Tuesdays and Fridays
the sorrowful mysteries

Wednesdays and Sundays
the glorious mysteries

13

The joyfu

mysteries

The annunciation

Mary answered the angel, 'Behold the handmaid of the Lord. Be it done unto me according to thy word.'

16

I want to know how to say yes to what God asks me.

Jesus, teach me to think of other people before I think of myself.

The visitation

When Mary arrived, Elizabeth kissed her and said to her, 'Blessed art thou among women and blessed is the fruit of thy womb.'

I want to be able to love and serve other people too. Who can I help today?

Mary, you brought joy to Elizabeth's house. Help me to spread joy and love around me.

The nativity

Mary gave birth to a son, her first-born. She wrapped him in swaddling-clothes and laid him in a manger.

Jesus is the most precious gift in the whole world!

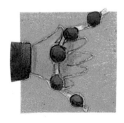

Mary, you gave birth to Jesus in a simple stable. Help me to look with love at all the poor people I meet.

The presentation of
Jesus in the temple

Simeon took the baby in
his arms and said, 'This
child will be a light to
enlighten all the nations.'

Do my eyes always
see what is beautiful
and good?

Mary, teach me to receive the
light of your son, Jesus.

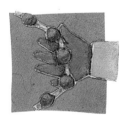

Finding Jesus
in the temple

Jesus said to Mary and Joseph, 'Why were you searching for me? Didn't you know I would be in my Father's house?'

I want to put Jesus at the centre of my life every day.

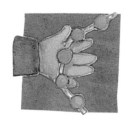

Mary, help me to listen to what Jesus is telling me in the Gospel and, like you, to keep it faithfully in my heart.

A PRAYER TO MARY

My soul glorifies the Lord,
my spirit rejoices in God, my Saviour.
He looks on his servant in her lowliness;
henceforth all ages will call me blessed.
The Almighty works marvels for me.
Holy his name!
His mercy is from age to age,
on those who fear him.
He puts forth his arm in strength
and scatters the proud-hearted.
He casts the mighty from their thrones
and raises the lowly.
He fills the starving with good things,
sends the rich away empty.
He protects Israel, his servant,
remembering his mercy,
the mercy promised to our fathers,
to Abraham and his sons for ever.

Glory be to the Father, and to the Son, and to the Holy Spirit.
As it was in the beginning, is now, and ever shall be,
world without end. Amen.

The Magnificat

21

The myster

s of light

The baptism of Jesus

And a voice came from heaven, 'This is my beloved son, in him I have put all my love.'

God loves me. I am his child and I love him.

Thank you Lord for being my father in heaven. Thank you mum and dad because I was baptised and am living in a Christian family.

The wedding at Cana

Mary said to the servants, 'Do whatever he tells you.'

How can I really listen to Jesus and do what he asks me?

Thank you Mary. You show me that the secret of happiness is to listen to the word of Jesus.

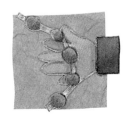

Jesus preaches about the kingdom

Jesus went throughout all Galilee, teaching in the synagogues and proclaiming the good news of the kingdom.

I too can follow Jesus and make him known to other people.

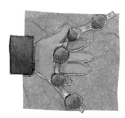

Jesus, you are so good, help me to be good too and to spread your message of love around me.

Jesus is transfigured

Jesus was transfigured
and his clothes shone
like lightning.

If I let myself be lit
up by Jesus, I will be
a light for the world.

Teach me, Mary, to look at Jesus
and listen to what he tells me in the
secret of my heart.

Jesus gives us the eucharist

Jesus took the bread, blessed it, broke it and gave it to his disciples saying, 'Take and eat. This is my body.'

When I receive the host, it is Jesus who lives in me.

Thank you, Jesus, for giving us your life. I pray for all the priests who give us your word and your body.

A PRAYER TO MARY

Holy Mary, mother of God,
preserve in me the heart of a child,
pure and transparent as a spring.
Obtain for me a simple heart
that does not brood over sorrows.
A heart generous in self-giving,
quick to feel compassion.
A faithful and generous heart
that forgets no favour,
and holds no grudge.
Give me a humble and gentle heart,
loving without asking any return.
A heart happy to lose itself in another heart,
that of your divine Son.

Léonce de Grandmaison

The sorro

ul mysteries

31

Jesus' prayer in the garden

Before he was arrested, Jesus said to his disciples, 'My soul is sorrowful unto death. Stay here and keep awake.' Then he went to pray to his father.

Do I know how to ask pardon for my sins and how to try not to do them again?

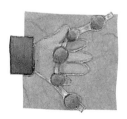

Jesus, forgive my sins. Give me the strength to change my heart to love you better and love other people better too.

Jesus is whipped

Jesus is beaten by the soldiers. Pilate orders them to take him away and whip him.

Jesus invites me to convert. How can I change my life and my heart?

Jesus, teach me to love with your heart so that I can grow in your love.

Jesus is crowned with thorns

The soldiers made a crown of thorns and put it on Jesus' head.

Like Jesus, I can reply to evil with good and to mockery with forgiveness.

Sweet Virgin Mary, teach me not to take revenge, to undo the bad things I have done and to comfort people who are suffering.

Jesus carries his cross

Then they took Jesus out, and he carried his cross.

Do I put up with
the great and small
sorrows of each
day without getting
discouraged?

Thank you, Jesus, for having carried
with your cross the weight of my sins.
Come and help all those who can't
carry their cross any more.

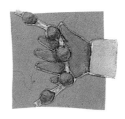

Jesus dies on the cross

After having suffered a lot, Jesus died on the cross, saying, 'Father, forgive them, they don't know what they're doing.'

How hard I find it to forgive those who hurt me and make me suffer!

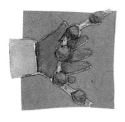

Thank you, Jesus. You gave your life for me. Forgive my sins as I would like to forgive those who have sinned against me.

A PRAYER TO MARY

Remember, O most loving Virgin Mary,
that it is a thing unheard of,
that anyone ever had recourse to your protection,
implored your help,
or sought your intercession,
and was left forsaken.
Filled therefore with confidence in your goodness,
I fly to you, O mother, Virgin of virgins.
To you I come, before you I stand,
a sorrowful sinner.
Despise not my poor words,
O Mother of the Word of God,
but graciously hear
and grant my prayer.
Amen.

The Memorare
Adapted from Saint Bernard

The glorio

38

mysteries

The resurrection of Jesus

Don't be afraid. I know you're looking for Jesus who was crucified. He isn't here. He has risen as he said.

I trust in Jesus. I know he is risen so that I can live with him for ever!

Jesus, I'm growing a little every day. Make my heart and my faith grow too, so I can bring the joy of your resurrection to the people around me.

Jesus goes up to heaven

After his resurrection,
Jesus blessed his disciples
and he withdrew from
them and was carried
up to heaven.

41

I don't see Jesus with my
eyes, but I know he is in
me and in all the people
who believe in him.

Thank you, Jesus, for your Church which
guides me and speaks to me about you.
Look after it as you look after me.

Pentecost

You will receive the Holy Spirit which will come down on you. You will be my witnesses to the ends of the earth.

The Spirit is God's love which he gives me. How will I welcome it?

Holy Spirit, come and give me your strength and your light so that I can carry your message of love and peace wherever I am.

Mary goes up to heaven

All generations will call me blessed, for the Almighty has done marvels for me.

I want to pray with my whole heart so that my prayer rises up to heaven, to Mary.

Mary, you are up in heaven.
Look after me, guide me, comfort me,
encourage me.

The crowning of Mary

A great sign appeared in heaven, a woman adorned with the sun, standing on the moon with twelve stars on her head for a crown.

Mary, queen of queens,
queen of peace,
queen of tenderness,
queen of obedience,
queen of humility...

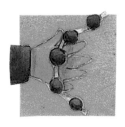

Mary queen of heaven, I offer you my heart. Let it become a star in your crown of glory!

A PRAYER TO MARY

In the presence of all the angels,
I choose you today, O Mary,
to be my mother and my queen.
I offer you my body and my soul.
I offer you all the good I have done
yesterday, today and tomorrow.
I offer you myself
so that you can lead me
in the love of God,
now and forever.

45

Adapted from St Louis-Marie Grignion de Montfort

Kno

Here are some places in
Europe where thousands of
pilgrims come to pray to Mary.
Do you know any others?

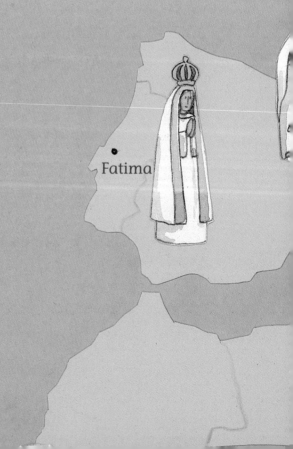

Fatima

Walsingham

Czestochowa

Beauraing

Paris

main

La Salette

des

47

CTS Children's Books

The Bible for little children, *by Maïte Roche*
(ISBN 1 86082 399 8 CTS Code CH 2)

The Gospel for little children, *by Maïte Roche*
(ISBN 1 86082 400 5 CTS Code CH 1)

The Rosary, *by Juliette Levivier*
(ISBN 186082 397 1 CTS Code CH 3)

The Way of the Cross, *by Juliette Levivier*
(ISBN 186082 398 X CTS Code CH 4)

The Rosary: Published 2006 by the Incorporated Catholic Truth Society, 40-46 Harleyford Road, London SE11 5AY. Tel: 020 7640 0042; Fax: 020 7640 0046; www. cts-online.org.uk. Copyright © 2006 The Incorporated Catholic Truth Society in this English language edition.

ISBN: 1 86082 397 1   CTS Code CH 3

Le rosaire (La prière des petits), by Juliette Levivier, illustrations by Anne Gravier, published 2006 by Edifa-Mame, 15-27 rue Moussorgski, 75018 Paris; ISBN Edifa 2-9145-8026-6; ISBN Mame 2-7289-1073-1. Copyright © Groupe Fleurus 2006.